Otherings

Otherings

poems by

Allison Cundiff

Golden Antelope Press
715 E. McPherson
Kirksville, Missouri 63501
2016

ISBN   978-1-936135-24-0 (1-936135-24-8)

Library of Congress Control Number: 2016940752

Published by:
Golden Antelope Press
715 E. McPherson
Kirksville, Missouri 63501

Available at:
Golden Antelope Press
715 E. McPherson
Kirksville, Missouri, 63501
Phone: (660) 665-0273
http://www.goldenantelope.com
Email: ndelmoni@gmail.com

M. Linn

For Camille, because she is my whole heart,
and because she told me
write it down, right now, before you forget.

Contents

Introduction

I'm no athlete, but I've heard that when you're at bat, you're supposed to try to see the ball *come in slow*. That's a great image. A hitter so focused he's able to manipulate his perception of time. I suppose there are several places in life where it would be nice to slow down the play, to savor what's coming. I regret the times I rushed.

Since Homer thought poetry offered some consolation for the loss of life, I thought to write about that, whittling down to the most important moments. I'm glad for words since they press people into paper so that something stays behind once we are gone. In her introduction to *Ariel* Frieda Hughes writes that her father was "dismayed to see their private business made the subject of a poem" (xiv). This makes sense. But I couldn't not write about the people in these poems. How do we cut our private business out of poetry without cutting the story out? It's a way to ask, "Is there anybody out there?"

Our lives are strange and ugly at times. The beautiful things have themselves. The more interesting times, the times I wish I could slow down like the pitcher's ball, have been the nights with too little sleep, the change of the late morning light after too much coffee, the wine with a newly returned friend, the hands shaking after a long flight. They've been night time with a thoughtful lover, getting to an age when friends die, all of everyone's babies, the look of men who don't have their own children, our children's bodies crowded everywhere, their fingers sticky, garden earth tracked inside on a shoe-print. They've been the relief of spring in everyone's shoulders, the woman carrying a brown paper bag with ingredients for morning sickness soup, how it felt to lean back in the chair, and to feel the woman's leg behind me, and her not moving her leg.

They've been playing all the dollar albums in low light, holding hands after you don't need to hold on any longer but you still do, sharing a cigarette and it tasting terrible, but still smoking it like a teenager. You want to savor the night you have the courage to tell the man you love, *please don't draw me in unless you intend to do good: I have to take care of other people.* And then there's the image left behind by someone long buried, the white paper I saved with the dried ring of coffee that his hands had held.

Part One

Birth of the Moon

There's a lip on the bottom corner
of the Harvest Moon.
Almost there like the one inside my body,
the anterior cervical lip, when I was
laboring my daughter here.
"Keep pushing," the nurse cooed,
her hand firm on my abdomen, as though she could
will me to open, to hold down that pain.

Meanwhile, my daughter.
Her little brown body a frond inside of me,
type O blood, her bones and teeth,
was channeling towards her own life.

Doctor Mary Grimm said, "pull your baby up to you,"
her dinner party interrupted by the hospital's needing
     call,
my blood on her scrubs, her clicking heels,
her earrings dangling above my pelvis,
her own three daughters at home.

I reached, pulling the baby from between my legs,
the pressure underwater primordial,
pulling like some cavewoman might have,
a knife between her teeth by a campfire.
I raised her from under her pink arms,
our hair the same, plastered wet,
her arrival serpentine, and not so unlike the moon,
round in the otherworldly.
Her slate eyes opened, locked into mine,
seeing before and after, a little
piece of God for me to nurse.

Warm cocoon tucked wet on swollen heartbeat,
swollen fingers, red scream, longest breath.
Thirst and then the bluecream milk,
honey ache in the electric air between us,
our nakedness in the dim warm light of evening.

Then my mother and her mother too,
The family in slow procession, the rosary beads in their
     fingers,

Passing the swaddled baby from woman to woman,
Welcome, we love you, we love you, little heart.

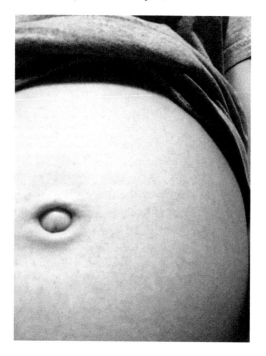

A. Cundiff

Dresser Change

Sometimes when I think about a man,
I like to think about his hands pulling his things out of
    his pockets
when he gets home, eager to get warm, to get his shoes
    off.

To maybe piss, to get a glass of bourbon.
And if I've loved him, I like to wonder how my body
    would fit
next to him on the bed, stepping out of my heels, my
    purse on the bed,
taking down my hair.

From outside,
standing in the wet grass watering the plants,
I see my two children
washing soap from their hands,
the incense curling between them,
one smiling at what the other's mouth says.

If only, for a moment I turned towards this:
I have you beside me,
both of us loving what we
have made together.
What would our life have been?

For a moment it stings,
but then dog's fur brushes my leg
as he chases something by the fence,
and the girls laugh, seeing me spill water in surprise.
and there is the *Times* still to read.

Lake (Haiku)

The fishing poles wait
leaning against the white side
of the too-still boat.

Spring

I can't believe it,
but the fig tree, whose
brown-fingered stalks
I half-abandoned by the brick
side of the house last week,
is green-budded at the tip today,
suddenly remembering itself
and the God it follows every spring.
It had been so small all winter,
all husk and gristle, with no
promise of second childishness.

It bloomed. I'm trying to think—
on the day I told that man

no to a future, my body crawling
backwards under the porch,
to pick dirt off
my cuticles and to chase worms.

It's late March again, and there's no time
to learn a man, his needs, to find out
if he snores, if he's kind when he's cold.
To memorize the way he takes his coffee
and which section of the *Times* he wants first.
I'd rather not.
There are the trees to repot
and seeds to watch sprout in the bright
basement corner.

F. DiPiazza

What Poor Feels Like

When my daughter was born, her father and I were both
   waiters.
If I didn't sell a bottle of good wine in a night,
I wouldn't have money for diapers.
I could wash the cloth ones, but I hated the drying,

cold wet, never clean white. And never all the way dry.

And even though he was always so mad at me, we tried.
We saved quarters. We made enough to shop
for dollar-carton milk.
And if you soak graham crackers in a low finger of milk,
a baby is happy. All gummy smiles and no words.

I think about the finger of milk sometimes these days
when there's finally money over dinner.

At night in winter there's a steel cold,
nervous, that feels the same way it feels when you're
    alone at a party,
wishing someone would just sit next to you on the floor,
    and you're 15,
or when the friend who called said she would be late,
    but then never comes
and it's an hour past bedtime.
What will you say to her at school Monday?
Or when the lack of sleep starts to kick in and you're
    sweating and in over your head,
knowing you're soon going to have to think about
the bills and the landline ringing about what's due
and he's still not home even though his shift ended four
    hours ago.

Dinner at *Taste* Restaurant

I had pulled my hair back severely.
My breasts were hidden.
One man ate too much from the community plate.
The man next to him spoke at a table of people about
    secret things.

I was troubled.
I ate chicken off the bone with my hands,
like I had been starved.

The woman across from me,
she used her linen to wipe my cheek.
She poured us both more wine.
Her husband did not notice.

F. DiPiazza

Being Six

The therapist asks about 6-7 year old me. She
asks her questions.
"How far was the fall?"
"Did you bleed?"
"Why don't you think you can remember anything?"
"Who drove you to the hospital?"
"Why don't you think they called an ambulance?"
"Why is there no hospital in that part of Missouri?"

I see myself there
very skinny
scraped raw by running too hard into life.

Library Girl

I see you holding
two slim books of Tennyson
against your belly.

You're one table over in plain clothes,
nothing itching your skin like my
plaid uniform skirt does to mine.
You've pulled a secret comic to read
in your lap while the poetry
sits falsely open on the table.
Your hair hangs over your cheeks.

If we could switch our bodies,
I could escape the shame of my skin
and crawl inside of yours. I'd wake
on a Thursday and take the school bus
to a brick building filled with plain-clothes
teachers instead of nuns. Maybe
the desk chairs would be comfortable.
Maybe I wouldn't worry about Hell so much,
even on school days. Maybe you'd start
to be nervous like I am and I'll wake up
without my heart racing like you do,
calm in your bedroom with the posters and
cream-colored sheets and
my new yard will be clear of tractors and heavy
chains. You can have those.

When we switch bodies, I will also like
your darker skin, free from burns and bites of
crawling country things. You can take mine,
feeling how a day in the sun with no shade trees
feels, feeling for once what it's like
to not walk around
parading your comfortable life.

First Crush

Mine was when I was four
at Parkway summer camp.
For a boy, but
it turned out to be a girl with a boy's hair cut.

And at the end of camp,
after a week of sharing orange drink from paper cups,
holding hands, and one kiss on my cheek,
he told me his name:
Amy.

I told her: I thought you were a boy
this whole time (my four year old heart pounding, sad
     then)
and she said, laughing, "I know"
and we were four years old.

A. Cundiff

Catholic School

No one waits
as still as
the child, sitting
hard against
the wood of
her punishment chair.

Mother

My lip is swollen.
Must have bumped it again.
I run my finger against it, tender,

in the waiting room with a concussion,
doctor-visit skinny.
Six or so, and had a bad fall from
a "jungle gym" the older kids called it,
and had these twitches that chased friends away except
for a good-intentioned Catholic girl
from school, and the one black girl.
We could safely be outcasts together.

Then to us our mothers were
like wild birds who still came
to feed us over and over,
beautiful still and not aware we knew we were becoming
    burdens to their beauty.

Our first grade class took a field trip to the Wonder Bread
    factory and my mother met us there. Taller than
any other woman and wafer thin with white winter arms,
    smiling to the mothers, talking with the nuns.
And there
I stood, twitching beside her, desperate to hold onto her
    hand
to be connected to something beautiful for once.

We pushed outside, our dimpled knuckles on the hori-
    zontal industrial bar of the door,
and somehow, she fell.

Very suddenly, I turned, too young for embarrassment.
And there she lay, beautiful on her awkward side
like Nike adjusting her sandal.
She laughed, accepted the hand from Sister Cristine,
and continued on to the car, her right hand smoothing
    the two loaves of bread
she would brown with cheese later that night for dinner.

Fig 2

The lawn boy turned twenty-three today.
I watched him grow up
a block down the street with two Siberian Huskies
who suffered so much in the summer that he
hand fed them fish from a tin, like some Alaskan Inuk
    would.
This morning he knocked on the door to ask about the
    fig tree.
Of the two I have, the one I had
the year I loved you
has not bloomed.
It stands in the yard like an old man, ridiculous in the
    sunlight,
and mocking me.
"Cut it down," I told him.
And "it's too late—" almost as an afterthought.
He didn't hear me, but pulled a hand saw
from the bed of his pickup
and I watched from the door,
his back bent in this small labor.

Nina Simone, *Live at Carnegie Hall*
is on the record player.
I wish you were on the bed still,
pawing at me while I put on my lipstick, the jade
ring you gave me, too big on my finger, your hands
pulling at my waist as I step into the heels.
That's what a husband does.
That's why he mows the grass and parks the car while
    she walks the children in.
For that moment.

Part Two

A. Cutraro

Little Havana

On the hottest day
we followed the Cubans down an alley,
one of those things my father would have pulled me back
    from, had he been there,
had he been.

And the metal bar-encased wooden door opened to
smoking brown-faced men.
"Fumar" they called it, and a girl with dreads
stood bored behind a grill, both hands occupied over
    pork and cilantro,
a cigarette ash limping from her long mouth.

The graffiti was in bold Havana wall orange and neon
    yellow
finally not crude since all of us were sweating, heat in
    our fingers
and between our kissing tongues.
What other color could there be, could there have ever
    been?

Then the car alarm, our running legs to the car,
interrupting the hand holding, while I sat on the busted
    out glass of the Chevy's window
to fill out the police report.
The cops were disappointed I didn't speak Spanish when
    they
looked over my over-browned daughter.
The sun heavy in their faces,
the r's in their mouths, asking "Why are you in Miami
    this weekend?"
and "Did you see anyone suspicious at all?"

Men outside all day have heat trapped in their skin.
The way the philosopher's skin smelled like good fish
    and the tobacco
he rolled between his fingers,
the fatigue green of his tank and his beard.
And how when he kissed me, the leash of his dog held
    between his fingers and mine,
he tasted hungry.
And then
lastly
when he took his left hand and held it hard
against my breastbone, eyes hooked into my face,
his palm pressing, beating,
like a crude Atlantic heart against my chest, not ashamed
    of things
like our clothes clinging in sweat,
the smell of smoke in between our teeth,
the stains on his from Havana youth, the none on mine,
I'll never see you again.
Let me have your tongue.
I'll never taste you again.
I'll bring you back before dawn.

A. Cutraro

Laylow

Do you ever think
about how
men

throw their bodies
into fire, into
caves of sulphur,
into
anything.

All that
western
suffering.

F. DiPiazza

Little Breakup Thoughts

You asked,
"any last thoughts?"
And there weren't then.
But now I remember,
little comings back,
little half forgottens.

The first is that my brother
spackled over the holes you made in the kitchen,
hanging that art
you knew I didn't like.
I am glad for that.

The second is that there's a quiet part
of the last ten seconds or so
of songs,
Beirut, Lou Reed, or Robyn Hitchcock
that I could never hear before through your talking.

It's not that they were your thoughts that were too loud
    for the room,
it's just that I never was interested in listening.
I am sorry for that.

There was that time I wanted
Korean, the clean-smelling counter and the greasy han-
    dle
on the diner door, two bells too,
But you couldn't get a beer there.
and "what was in that dish anyway," you had asked.
If I were alone, I could have found
my place in the corner
with the book and no
conversation to agonize over.
and looking up to see the cook reading too, not watching
    me.

Standing, on Delmar Boulevard, you called me a fool
for loving the dead.
Maybe so. But after awhile
I stopped trying to make you see
love can't ever breathe in the cornering way,
the way the deer is after she accidentally
steps on a trap meant for smaller game,
waiting with watery eyes, adrenaline heart,
for whatever different-smelling animal to come and eat
    her
in the cold bright
of a southern Missouri day.

A. Cundiff

Dickens and You

Pip in the graveyard.
For what's in your heart pockets,
I'm holding you upside down.

A. Cundiff

In Mycenae

The potter smiles,
his hand holds clay in a slip.
His grey gaze on mine.

Hard Rain

I ran
hard
in the rainslick
street, calling
the dog
who had run away again.

I was in tennis shoes
with no socks.
I was trying not to think of the what if of our dog's body
motionless in the road.
What would I tell my kids?
It was me who had left the door cracked for the smell of
    the rain.

There was that morning on the farm that the horse
stomped the life out of the pregnant beagle.
After, her face was still, blood-filled mouth open,
but her belly still moved with life.

I left the next part to my father and brother,
walking hard, seven miles down the dusty road
where no truck passed until my father's
hours later to find me.
Neither of us spoke on the ride home.

Now, though, there's no man to call for those sorts of
    things.
I suppose it was time. I could handle it. I'd been
through childbirth, after all.
I called out her name in the rain.
I slipped a bit on the colorful oil puddle,
seeing my reflection staring back at me,
my hair wet.
My nose started to bleed again
after the sidewalk
turned to grass.

I saw her. I whistled quick.
She looked up, not unlike a deer would from grazing,
and froze, thought about it, then came.

She trotted happily to me.

And with the dark patches
of blood drying on my wrists,
over my cold fingers,
I walked her home.

F. DiPiazza

Cobblestone Skin

Lines on your brown palms
like the sun still setting there,
face of the sunflower turning up
to find the light.

My hands are pale red,
burns and freckles.
A girlfriend once called my skin
milk and roses,
but that image is
prettier than I am.

F. DiPiazza

Palermo

Butter lettuce stand.
Tomatoes on vine, so ripe,
eating them like apples.

A. Cundiff

A. Cundiff

Valentine's Day

I suppose
the question I had
most, over and over, watching you
on the floor
with pipe in
your hands,
was where you were
all those years
growing up,
that somehow brought you to me
on my floor
repairing my plumbing

on Valentine's Day.
But I
could
not ask, so I
traced the
line of your spine with
my foot, toes
painted
red.

A man working is
quiet, as you were.
Your mind
taking you here and there,
thinking about the way
things work together, about the small
choices you made
at 10, 20, 35. About
the blood, red in your mouth
when that one day
your hammer hit your top lip.

Then breathing you
in when you finally came to
bed, the sawdust washed
from your hair, your tired breath,
hands rough from work, and taking them into mine,
two hands I had waited forever for.

A. Cundiff

Theo

Shadow tips cover the ancient gate
where you told me to wait,
not to be late.

Rusting copper bore into
limestone looking as old as it was new,
fragments of Corinthians.

My hand warm over where yours
would be, your dusted jacket.
The lines around your eyes deeper,
talking of your
grown children and
where you wanted to die, in these mountains,
screaming your secrets.

A. Cundiff

A. Cundiff

Nothing Feels As Good

At the Record Exchange I looked for the Sam Cooke
in the dollar stack of albums in the twenty-minute win-
    dow of time I had,
the plastic edges bumping the cut on my thumb again
    and again,
that's you.

All the morning alarms and trips to the grocery
and pauses at the sink looking up while I brush my teeth,
the bright light showing my face too much in the morn-
    ing.
That's you too.

And I just have to say that nothing feels as good
as the man that wants you with nothing else in the way.
Not his ex, not his fantasies. But first match,
knowing it is doomed, but loving anyway.
That's it.

The best day is always Saturday.
If it's good, it's not too sunny.
No school for two days.

One Saturday I swung too high on a swing with two
    metal chains
attached to a rocking set next to my house growing up.
When you went so high you could hang your head back
    on the upswing
and see the yellow snowplows resting on grass
that later my father would take a weed-eater to.
On the way up would be the not too bright sun if you
    were lucky.
And then the squeak of the swing, and your scarred
    knees pushed together,
not yet touched by any man, the belly flipping,
your long hair grazing the ground.

One day
somehow, I fell.
I don't remember until after, the fuzzy ache,
piercing, my legs numb.
I suppose, that's you too.

Rome

You really love the person you think about
when you're walking in Rome,
your boots catching on cobblestone.

I wrote our names on a lock,
"Keith, Allison,"
now clasped on the Ponte Vecchio
and tossed the key into the Arno.

I saw your eyes
in passersby, thinking about

having a baby with you,
thinking about how your skin felt
after a day in the sun.

Bill

Bill V., former almost-deacon of the Russian Orthodox
    Church,
love for his wife unchanged after she birthed three ba-
    bies,
lover of Homer but quiet about it, won't lay the book
    out,
even if there are scholars about, 19th-century unfussed,
    Bill.

Both our heads down passing
too-loud talkers, drinking strong coffee,
walking once, I saw we were both carrying copies of
    Lattimore,
worn from too much touching.

Seven months later we loaded
clusters of teenagers on a plane to Athens.
In the pouring rain
he smiled when I ask him to get into the picture,
his glasses fogging.

Part Three

F. DiPiazza

Climax Springs

When debris hits the bottom of the boat,
it feels like a low bass drum banging from
under water, under the rib cage.
You feel it before you hear it.
And when you're steering,
like when you're in love,
you're terrified.

I'm not sad because you left me.
I just don't understand how you keep choosing this
over "being some bored house cat at the window,"
you said, talking to me as you walked away,
your face turned left over your shoulder saying,

"And it's your own fault."

The man who had had the stroke
said "Don't go to the western dam,"
his face pulled down hard
like there was an invisible fish hook. And he was right.
The bark was heavybrown in the water from weeks of
soddy rain.
The logs jutted up vertically, ready to take out the un-
derside of your boat,
ready to sink you into that green pond water lake.
So I pulled off for a beer.

In the Red Fox Tavern off MM 52
the man in the NASCAR teeshirt was singing,
I like the way your sparkling earrings lay,
girls whose mothers would call them "a little heavy"
crowded the bar,
and all the things that made me hide so long ago came
crashing back,
my father's great big arms reduced to heavy skin
and the itching scar on his tricep from the time he was
shot at the A&W
in 1959 because the guy pulled in too close to the right
of his Chevy
and because he was the kind of man who wouldn't stand
for that;
purple blood staining the red upholstery of the driver's
seat so much
so that he sold it.

The woman with the too-long fingers and an oversized
shirt
was sitting with a cigarette. I longed for one
though I hadn't smoked in 17 years.
One month late for my period, my cramps aching through
wet jean shorts.

And even though I'm writing this at work two days later,
I don't feel it any less than I did.
All the wet shame coming back.

And I'm still, always, in charge of the kids,
all their tangled hair,

all the carrying on with the litters of kittens, the sun-
    burns, the crying for candies,
and their firm warm bodies after hours in the sun,
the sunburn a pink line in the part of their scalps.
The smallest falling asleep in the hot sun against my
    chest,
being thirsty always. Even through the boat bumping,
the motor spurting arcs of water over their bodies, sleep-
    ing,
the suits too colorful, child ridiculous.

It was the kind of day that you turn the boat around for
    fireworks
even if everyone is sunsick because
Venus is so bright and because summer is library book-
    time over
and because the girls' dad never called back and because
you really won't know what you'll do if you are pregnant
    after all
and because of the sweetness of no work tomorrow and
    the stars,
so pretty in the dark sky, the boats all angled like all of
    Van Gogh's
in some French river he looked at through his frantic
    night eyes.

A. Cundiff

A. Cundiff

Love

The most terrifying word to say
is a chain link lingual curse
of forever and I'll never and always.
Waiting to be broken, break me. Waiting to hold me
down like some brownfurred Missouri animal
with your foot on my neck,
in your heavy boots, coat carhartt beige and aged,
just to say you've trapped me in
your metal jaws while you go off hunting for other game,
my leg broken at the knee,
blood on the grass of my whole terrified life.
Please, not again.

What is not as terrifying is the woman behind the Delta
counter
with the watery brown eyes
after I've missed the connecting flight.

"No flight until tomorrow at 7 am" but also,

"there's a flight home for you in 20 minutes, no cost for
  that,"
her finger a brown line pointing a mere walk across the
  terminal,
one fast paced walk away from you, back back to where
  I've come,
so easy to run, and a glass of Cabernet on the plane
  maybe
and I am back to the barking dogs and quiet tooth brush-
  ing at 1 am.

There's no magic voice or sign
other than the blister
that appeared all of a sudden
on my left heel, and the
hope that you meant it when you wrote me *je t' aime.*

"I'll take the 7 am."

So then she says, "I'm sorry, honey,"
and "here's a little blanket for the night."
The small action steps of moving toward you, the micro
  correctness
of you making me laugh
despite the nine hours ahead of me.

Then slightly more than a day later
Sitting on a bench in Queens
Putting a Band-Aid on my heel,
I look over to see
Your gaze on me, you say
something about my eyes in the sun,
I can't even remember.
You held my hand
all day, until you finally
let it go again.

A. Cundiff

Curmudgeon Bar

The Friday bartender at Kenn's Broome Street is WASP
handsome
as though he's got a football under the bar
they are waiting to toss to someone.

He'll serve us, but he'll be in a little bit of a hurry
to get back to the cheerleaders lined up behind the bar

or the stacks of hundred dollar bills, or the cars with big
    quiet motors—
all the clean white good looks, the very straight teeth.

On Friday, October 30th, the Mets played the Royals
in the third game of the World Series.
My date ordered a bottle of Malbec and a cup of coffee.

And it was one of those surgery conversations you don't
    move from
because you need to hear exactly what is said at each
    moment,
and also because there are 50 working-class men behind
    you
patting your back whenever New York does something
    on the field.

The Yale-tall bartender tossed his dish towel over his
    long shoulder
and smiled as he refilled the coffee.

A. Cundiff

Joe's Shanghai

You were starving by the time
we got to Chinatown,
the crease in your brow
deeper in hunger,
your stare at the waiter who lingered in delivery of the
    dumplings,
his absurd Halloween hat falling off as he rushed stacks
    of the delicacy to everyone but us.

I liked the way your irritation slipped out, simply

"He can't even look me in the eye," you mentioned al-
   most to yourself.
You got mad for the first time in front of me, maybe mad
   like
you had been in front of your mother, your wife, or the
   one before,
and now me, later in your life.
Tucked in the corner of a round table with strangers,
you filled my tea over and over,
your mind somewhere else.

Lovers should eat, especially
new lovers. I knew better.
You did too.
But what should I have done?
The clock was between us, time pulling me back. No
   time for anything but yesterday's water.

Waiting outside as you ordered
black coffee, I saw your mouth practicing the Cantonese
I still can't bear to hear.
Though it sounded nice
in your voice, finally, no accent attached to it,
a courtesy instead of a secret.
The way your lips
pursed to blow on the drink,
not too different from the kissing
we had just fallen into
one day before, our bodies
long in a too-warm bed
with a view you chose,
of the sandstone of Brooklyn bridge.

How To Properly Eat A Burger

A burger is best eaten when you're finally off the clock.
When you have the sort of job that requires you to know
the stiffness of a timecard,
all the punched grooves of your life
lined up until payday.

A burger is served differently
at Balthazar on Spring Street.
The white-clothed tables all taken,
I used my Ozark elbow
to get us a spot at the bar,
getting a protest in Russian from
a woman in a fur coat.
But you had told me that I had to be assertive in the city
or else I wouldn't even be able to get across the street.

A burger at Balthazar can be served
with a soft-boiled egg.
I stared at it while a couple next to us drank champagne.
But all I could think about while you cut it
in half with a *foie gras* knife,
was the feel of a burger with a punchcard-tired body,
at Diner 54 on South Baltimore, ten miles south of Novinger.

二〇一二年一月二十八日 (28 January 2012)

Monday mornings should be difficult
because of being weekend tired, because of having two
Sunday drinks with your out-of-town friends instead of
    just one,
because the full week is before you,
because you want to stay in bed until the sun comes
    through your curtains.

Monday mornings should not be
a time when the phone rings
and a voice tells you
that your lover has died.
That phone call belongs to Friday nights.
Friday's wildness can take it.
Friday has the time, has the car ready,
has you able to survive hearing it.

When the phone rings on a Monday
I answer it in a moment between classes,
and after I walk straight out of the classroom—
pushing through hundreds of bodies in the hallway,
no one moving out of the way fast enough—
I realize I have forgotten my coat
as I'm walking in the steel cold to the car.

In the two-lane road everyone else is driving too slowly
with their friends down the street, alive, and NPR
is cooing about a recipe with living people talking
and maybe they should fix the lights so that when
someone dies you really can just drive through them
and everyone sees you and thinks, *oh God, I hope
everything is okay.*

There's a time, after you die,
when people go through your things.
Your most private drawers will be turned
inside out. That Monday they found the note I wrote
    you,
the private one,
and suddenly it was clutched in your sister's hand.
If you die in your bed, your body is taken away,

but your crumpled sheets will be left in your unmade
    bed,
before someone tucks them back.
On that Monday I learned that when you die, the paramedics
    don't
straighten out your sheets or touch anything
other than the body. They also tell you, "what we are
    taking away is not him,
this is just what's left behind." They can say those things
    to you.

At the memorial dinner
they didn't know what to do with me.
I was at the table farthest away
from the family. When, per your family's customs,
we were served plate after plate of your favorite dishes,
the sesame and ginger stuck in my throat,
chopsticks shaking in my hands.
They all spoke Cantonese
and looked me over, and my father turned to me,
he had come along so I wouldn't walk in alone,
and he turned to me and steadied my hand.

His ex-wife left me a bag of his things. There were
a few books in the bag, a half-eaten jar of Nutella the
    kids had split,
a tablecloth with a stain, and my favorite:
slips of paper with notes you had written to yourself.
Half thoughts, half in Chinese, half in your fast English
    cursive,
the real treasure that the others had cast away, worth
    nothing to them.

I have them tacked next to my bed,
some proof that before the great nothing of what you
    are now
that you thought about what you needed from the gro-
    cer,
that you were low on soy and olive oil,
that you wanted to live.

A. Cundiff

Trust Me

How do I know you?
Aut Deus, aut malus homo.
I thought I could help.

After Your Lover Dies

Knuckle to my mouth
sucking away the blood that's left
after running it
against the stone
mossy and ancient,
mile after mile.

Pickup Parked Outside

There was his coat first.
Dri Duck in beige past worn,
flannel underneath that, blue.
Below the flannel there was a white, round at the neck
cotton undershirt. Smelling like lumber at the collar.
Too many washes had faded it. Maybe it was the one
I wore to bed that winter.
Under the white undershirt there was human skin.
The age of his skin,
my age now.

But let's go back for a second.
The browned skin, maybe a little like leather from a life
    outside,
strong and a little too thin, a little distracted,
a man who never hurried when he walked,
as though every step was meant to be at that pace.

Under the skin was a rib cage that had formed inside his
    mother
forty something years before,
and under that,
(I claim him, fuck you world, fuck you)
a muscle, complicated, beating, broken by love and other
    women.

Confused, like a child, his eyes shooting up, looking
    right, closing then,
hard, sad he would be found, making sure it was his
    friend who found him,
the sound of a mower in the distance, crows too.
And then underwater with blood pooling, over his chest,
    my chest now,
waterfalls full of him everywhere.
Now I toast with it,
every meal, every night
"Let me walk you home."

Cove in Spring

The fisherman stood calfdeep in the cove, the mossed
    underside
of the fishing boat held hard, minnows
darting from each of the muddying steps,
his fishing boots disrupting the brown freshwater.

The smell of catfish was strong by the lines.
"They'll cut you if they can," he said, looking not at me.
The acreage around the lake showed more brown leaf
    coverage
than it did tree lines. No green yet.
The wood burning stove kept you warm only if you stayed
close enough for your cheeks to get too hot.

He kneeled in front of it, feeding
its black maw the wood he had chopped
that morning, pockets of sweat under his arms
though there was still frost on the Chevy's windshield.

So grateful for the heat,
so much so we didn't move back,
even through the spitting sparks lit out on his long arms.

F. DiPiazza

Stardust

Once he dropped his voice
down to a whisper,
all the edges gone finally.
His eyes looked a hard line
to above him where a white crack
inched along to
wherever it would go.
Come to collect, I suppose

on years of too much alone.

Say the right words and a man can
collect a woman's eye locked
to hold his as strongly as his
holds hers. His hands collect
her cold breasts in his hands
until, like a baker's bread, she is warm,
wet under his touch, whose arm
suddenly belongs to her chest,
his heartbeat breaking through her
skin, a clock ticking down
minutes, she does not think,
does not remember the electric
call of first love, only this now,
the slower and more tepid coupling,
his breath, a bear's in cold sleep on
her collar now, and his collar
where she kissed him just before,
the fold of skin beneath his lip
where she will grow smaller,
smaller, grow backwards,
him too, body below body,
recoiled into their own
star dust where millions
of years before their bodies
curled poised, surrounded
by quiet black matter,
waiting to be born.

Shame

No shame in a dog's
gnawing of his bone.
Or his watery jowls
lifting up from the green lake water.
No shame in the men's
faces looking over us.
(Keith looked once. Before
I was his, I stood in a faded bikini,
my hair piled on my head, carrying

a baby above pond scum into
warm Missouri summer water.
I looked up for him, a story above
held on rickety boards.
He had gripped the side of the wood.
I knew he would watch over,
I wouldn't fall).

No shame in the flies
landing in my bourbon.
No shame in that one kid
who chooses the viola
over the violin.

No shame in the scrappy
unkillable destitute
who stands next to the sign on Delmar
forbidding "aggressive begging."

No shame in my heart
to cling to the dead.

Dear

In my dream you're walking
with a book the size of something
a gentleman would carry
in his pocket, no bigger than
a handkerchief, and it's nothing
unusual, as though men still carried
books around still.

When I see you at that moment
I know you'll die, but you don't.
I try to tell you but you won't look up from your book.
This terrible irony, I'm an older and sadder Cassandra,
and Agamemnon laughs.

How sad it is that in all those moments of kissing you,
I didn't realize that there would a time when it would
    stop.
I would have pressed each one into my memory some-
    how.

You told me that what we could be

was something you read about once but couldn't remem-
ber.
The woman loves without quitting. The man
works with his hands.
And I was trying to listen to the words but your mouth
was moving,
the mouth that has tasted mine over
and I was too busy with all the textbooks.
Over and over, the sticking guilt. These are the things
that women think about
after their lovers die.

When we are dead, it won't matter
how nice our voices sounded when we answered the
phone *hello.*
It won't matter that once you had held my body in the
low light
of that morning in LaPlata.
I would be the last to remember, and I'll be gone then
too.
No children to tell about how it felt to run my fingers
Through a man's hair,
his head's rested breath on my belly.

J. Blair

The Body

Of course it would snow the day after you died.
I was driving east on Manchester, fast
enough to make me realize I was very alone in the car,
alone on the road since it was just Tuesday and people
were
tired and indoors warming their bodies.

I was also alone when I walked in the funeral parlor,
large hallways empty of crying people with many locked
doors and
I thought I could open any one of them and see all the
bodies that were there,
hidden from us, as if we couldn't feel them, as if we
didn't see them still.
Rose fragrance to mask the stench of death,
shit art hanging above the mirrors as though it could
comfort.
There was one woman there and there was me.
They had stayed open a few more minutes because his
son had called.

If I owned a funeral parlor, I would make it as empty as
possible.
Nothing inside.
Don't think cheap prints will cut the black out of
anyone's chest.

The woman who took my name and license asked my
"relation to the deceased." The family had been there
earlier.
"Why was I there so late?" She was wearing expensive
shoes.
I told her "friend" since they had no word for "lover"
on the sheet I filled out.
They had no word for "woman his ex-wife didn't want
around,
still don't know why, I was always polite."
There could have been a word for "girlfriend, maybe,
driver of our kids."
What is the word for "lover" in Cantonese?

Probably three pronunciations, and if I said it incorrectly
I'd inadvertently call you a horse or something.

I remember when I looked up "sexy" in Cantonese on
    Google
and said it to you after you got home from work.
You were hanging up your jacket, and you laughed and
    laughed
since I had accidentally called you something akin to a
    street-walker
and we drank Cabernet on your
big white bed and you tried to teach me more words
and said I was doing well, your voice rising,
and I loved the sound of you happy.
We were a little drunk.
That's the night you asked me to marry you.

This woman's shoes made no sound on the carpet.
This woman walked in front of me for some time
then opened the door in a semi-grand gesture, the door
    at the end of the long vacant hallway, which had
    been locked, and asked me, "are you ready?"
I told her I was. But why was it locked? Why all those
    little things.
But what if I had said no?
How do we know beforehand if we are ready?

Days before we were sleeping, hearts beating, in bed.
Days before you were walking, your arms and legs were
    moving.
Days before your fingers held babies as you vaccinated
    them,
checking their new limbs in the hospital. "Newborns,"
    you always called them.
Your most recent was a girl, the day before you died,
    "perfect, really" you called her.

"He's there, down the stairs" she said, and her hand rose
    as if
gesturing to a stage. And I wanted to say, no that's not
    him.
He is holding a newborn right now. He is picking up
    dinner from Lulu,

he is driving behind me home to be sure
I get in okay.

But does she get those questions all the time?
Questions like, "who washed his body?" "Why couldn't
    it have been me?"
Would she have put my name in a book? A crazy lady,
    I know, I know,
I don't grieve the right way. I get all Greek tragedy in-
    side and
nobody wants to see that. I'd save it for the drive home.
So pushed my fingernails into my palm. I bit my left
    inside lip.

I stood by his right side. The side he couldn't hear out
    of.
Had he not been dead, I could have spoken to him
and he wouldn't have heard me.
Sometimes in bed I would whisper, "I love you,"
something I could never say during waking hours,
but I'd whisper into his right ear and he wouldn't hear,
he would keep on reading in bed, his feet under the blan-
    ket.
Had he heard me he would have been surprised, looking
    over.
Because I never said it,
because I was cold-hearted and distant he thought,
and too difficult to access.
Well, I said it then, and, same as always,
he didn't hear me and he went on being dead.

And it was all too late since his body
was some leftover and would soon be
burned into bone dust to be put in an urn for
his spot back in Hong Kong to be with his mother.

And on the way home I saw his son run out of a restau-
    rant,
his hair getting wet in the rain, and he came to the car
    window and stared at my face
and I told him to put his hood up because I could see
the snow collecting in iridescent drops on his straight
    black hair,

dropping onto his cheeks and then darkening the grey
    of his sweatshirt.
And as he raised the hood I saw your eyes, your fingers,
your mouth, and I drove home through the wet snow,
my chest feeling like there was someone standing on it.
And when I got back home the kids ran inside from the
    rain,
and I stood in the yard for a long time with the excuse
    that I was bringing in the yard can,
but what I really wanted to feel was the water dropping
    onto my hair,
down over my eyes onto my cheeks and darkening my
    sweater,
whose color I have forgotten now.

J. Blair

A. Cundiff

Judy Loves Steve

Judy holds a toddler in each of her arms.
The small one arches his back,
his blonde home-cut hair
like stalks between his eyes.

She's tired, but baby care makes her happy.
She's happy too to talk about the man
who made her back-to-back pregnant:

We met in the laundry room.
Basement level, salt light
brick wall, coins in pocket.

I was wearing my dirty clothes.
Over the thump of the washer,
I didn't hear him come in.
He put in his Billybob teeth.
He made me laugh.

He kept coming up to my room.
"I live on 2 if you need anything!"

The next day then.
"Hey, I'm just down on 2.
If ever you need me."

Before Dinner

I am eating an olive,
my right hip against your
sink. You're
standing two feet away
from me and I can hear
the steady drip at the faucet
that has bothered you for months.
It makes me think
of you washing up at the basin
before you leave for work.
Those mornings I'd just watch
you from bed, you ten minutes late,
fussing over the tie, tucking in
your shirt as you leaned to kiss me goodbye.
It wouldn't have worked out anyway, I tell myself.

Maybe you'd let me sit on the tub and watch you shave
and you wouldn't think what your fucking department
      chair would think
of me in your bed.
Or what we had written that he pretended he hadn't
      read.
But how to crawl out from under all that?
And I'm wondering what's best to do with the olive pit.
Holding it in the right pocket of my cheek.

Today

Midway through Act I.v,
Romeo refers to Juliet as a "holy shrine"
and the girls swoon and the boys snicker
and say yeah yeah "but no one talks like that"
and I think about our Missouri strip malls.
Of course we don't.

Skinny David asks, "did Romeo see shrines all the time?
Maybe his moms taught him about the shrine growing
      up quiet in them,
like telling him *shh, hold my hand,*

don't touch, maybe his moms said that the same way she said
don't touch the girls and be nice."

And then, dragging his sleeve across his runny nose,
"Ms. Cundiff, when did people talk like this?
And then, "Ms. Cundiff, when did they stop?"
And then, "Ms. Cundiff, how did Shakespeare die?"
And then, "Ms. Cundiff, how do I get good with words like that?"

M. Linn

Credits

"Little Havana" first appeared in *The Chariton Review*.

Photography by John Blair, Allison Cundiff, Belinda Cundiff (back cover image), Andrew Cutraro, Frank DiPiazza, Dan Haas (front cover image) and Mark Linn.

CPSIA information can be obtained
at www.ICGtesting.com
Printed in the USA
LVOW05s2137070616
491649LV00009B/27/P